Successful Methods

of

Public Speaking

SUCCESSFUL METHODS

of

PUBLIC SPEAKING

GRENVILLE KLEISER

FORMERLY INSTRUCTOR IN PUBLIC SPEAKING AT
YALE DIVINITY SCHOOL, YALE UNIVERSITY.

AUTHOR OF *"How to Speak in Public," "Great Speeches and How to Make Them," "Complete Guide to Public Speaking," "How to Build Mental Power," "Talks on Talking,"* etc., etc.

ſerenity
Publishers, LLC
ROCKVILLE, MARYLAND
2009

ISBN: 978-1-60450-590-0

Published by Serenity Publishers
An Arc Manor Company
P. O. Box 10339
Rockville, MD 20849-0339
www.SerenityPublishers.com
Printed in the United States of America/United Kingdom

Contents

PREFACE

As you carefully study the successful methods of public speakers, as briefly set forth in this book, you will observe that there is nothing that can be substituted for personal sincerity. Unless you thoroughly believe in the message you wish to convey to others, you are not likely to impress them favorably.

It was said of an eminent British orator, that when one heard him speak in public, one instinctively felt that there was something finer in the man than in anything he said.

Therein lies the key to successful oratory. When the truth of your message is deeply engraved on your own mind; when your own heart has been touched as by a living flame; when your own character and personality testify to the innate sincerity and nobility of your life, then your speech will be truly eloquent, and men will respond to your fervent appeal.

GRENVILLE KLEISER.

New York City,
August, 1919.

Successful Methods of Public Speaking

You can acquire valuable knowledge for use in your own public speaking by studying the successful methods of other men. This does not mean, however, that you are to imitate others, but simply to profit by their experience and suggestions in so far as they fit in naturally with your personality.

All successful speakers do not speak alike. Each man has found certain things to be effective in his particular case, but which would not necessarily be suited to a different type of speaker.

When, therefore, you read the following methods of various men, ask yourself in each case whether you can apply the ideas to advantage in your own speaking. Put the method to a practical test, and decide for yourself whether it is advisable for you to adopt it or not.

REQUIREMENTS OF EFFECTIVE SPEAKING

There are certain requirements in public speaking which you and every other speaker must observe. You must be grammatical, intelligent, lucid, and sincere.

These are essential. You must know your subject thoroughly, and have the ability to put it into pleasing and persuasive form.

But beyond these considerations there are many things which must be left to your temperament, taste, and individuality. To compel you to speak according to inflexible rules would make you not an orator but an automaton.

The temperamental differences in successful speakers have been very great. One eminent speaker used practically no gesture; another was in almost constant action. One was quiet, modest, and conversational in his speaking style; another was impulsive and resistless as a mountain torrent.

It is safe to say that almost any man, however unpretentious his language, will command a hearing in Congress, Parliament, or elsewhere, if he gives accurate information upon a subject of importance and in a manner of unquestioned sincerity.

You will observe in the historical accounts of great orators, that without a single exception they studied, read, practised, conversed, and meditated, not occasionally, but with daily regularity. Many of them were endowed with natural gifts, but they supplemented these with indefatigable work.

WELL-KNOWN SPEAKERS AND THEIR METHODS

Chalmers

There is a rugged type of speaker who transcends and seemingly defies all rules of oratory. Such a man was the great Scottish preacher Chalmers, who was without polished elocution, grace, or manner, but who through his intellectual power and moral earnestness thrilled all who heard him.

He read his sermons entirely from manuscripts, but it is evident from the effects of his preaching that he was not a slave to the written word as many such speakers have been. While he read, he retained much of his freedom of gesture and physical expression, doubtless due to familiarity with his subject and thorough preparation of his message.

John Bright

You can profitably study the speeches of John Bright. They are noteworthy for their simplicity of diction and uniform quality of directness. His method was to make a plain statement of facts, enunciate certain fundamental principles, then follow with his argument and application.

His choice of words and style of delivery were most carefully studied, and his sonorous voice was under such complete control that he could speak at great length without the slightest fatigue. Many of his illustrations were drawn from the Bible, which he is said to have known better than any other book.

Lord Brougham

Lord Brougham wrote nine times the concluding parts of his speech for the defense of Queen Caroline. He once told a young man that if he wanted to speak well he must first learn to talk well. He recognized that good talking was the basis of effective public speaking.

Bear in mind, however, that this does not mean you are always to confine yourself to a conversational level. There are themes which demand large treatment, wherein vocal power and impassioned feeling are appropriate and essential. But what Lord Brougham meant, and it is equally true to-day, was that good public speaking is fundamentally good talking.

Edmund Burke

Edmund Burke recommended debate as one of the best means for developing facility and power in public speaking. Himself a master of debate, he said, "He that wrestles with us strengthens our nerves and sharpens our skill. Our antagonist is our helper. This amiable conflict with difficulty obliges us to have an intimate acquaintance with our subject, and compels us to consider it in all its relations. It will not suffer us to be superficial."

Burke, like all great orators, believed in premeditation, and always wrote and corrected his speeches with fastidious care. While such men knew that inspiration might come at the moment of speaking, they preferred to base their chances of success upon painstaking preparation.

Massillon

Massillon, the great French divine, spoke in a commanding voice and in a style so direct that at times he almost overwhelmed his hearers. His pointed and personal questions could not be evaded. He sent truth like fiery darts to the hearts of his hearers.

I ask you to note very carefully the following eloquent passage from a sermon in which he explained how men justified themselves because they were no worse than the multitude:

"On this account it is, my brethren, that I confine myself to you who at present are assembled here; I include not the rest of men, but consider you as alone existing on the earth. The idea which occupies and frightens me is this: I figure to myself the present as your last hour and the end of the world; that the heavens are going to open above your heads; our Savior, in all His glory, to appear in the midst of the temple; and that you are only assembled here to wait His coming; like trembling criminals on whom the sentence is to be pronounced, either of life eternal or of everlasting death; for it is vain to flatter yourselves that you shall die more innocent than you are at this hour. All those desires of change with which you are amused will continue to amuse you till death arrives, the experience of all ages proves it; the only difference you have to expect will most likely be a larger balance against you than what you would have to answer for at present; and from what would be your destiny were you to be judged this moment, you may almost decide upon what will take place at your departure from life. Now, I ask you (and connecting my own lot with yours I ask with dread), were Jesus Christ to appear in this temple, in the midst of this assembly, to judge us, to make the dreadful separation betwixt the goats and sheep, do you believe that the greatest number of us would be placed at His right hand? Do you believe that the number would at least be equal? Do you believe there would even be found ten upright and faithful servants of the Lord, when formerly five cities could not furnish so many? I ask you. You know not, and I know it not. Thou alone, O my God, knowest who belong to Thee. But if we know not who belong to Him, at least we know that sinners do not. Now, who are the just and faithful assembled here at present? Titles and dignities avail nothing, you are stript of all these in the presence of your Savior. Who are they? Many sinners who wish not to be converted; many more who wish, but always put it off; many others who are only converted in appearance, and again fall back to their former courses. In a word, a great number who flatter themselves they have no occasion for conversion. This is the party of the reprobate. Ah! my brethren, cut off from this assembly these four classes of sinners, for they will be cut off at the great day. And now appear, ye just! Where are ye? O God, where are Thy chosen? And what a portion remains to Thy share."

Gladstone

Gladstone had by nature a musical and melodious voice, but through practise he developed an unusual range of compass and variety. He could sink it to a whisper and still be audible, while in open-air meetings he could easily make himself heard by thousands.

He was courteous, and even ceremonious, in his every-day meeting with men, so that it was entirely natural for him to be deferential and ingratiating in his public speaking. He is an excellent illustration of the value of cultivating in daily conversation and manner the qualities you desire to have in your public address.

John Quincy Adams

John Quincy Adams read two chapters from the Bible every morning, which accounted in large measure for his resourceful English style. He was fond of using the pen in daily composition, and constantly committed to paper the first thoughts which occurred to him upon any important subject.

Fox

The ambition of Fox was to become a great political orator and debater, in which at last he succeeded. His mental agility was manifest in his reply to an elector whom he had canvassed for a vote, and who offered him a halter instead. "Oh thank you," said Fox, "I would not deprive you of what is evidently a family relic."

His method was to take each argument of an opponent, and dispose of it in regular order. His passion was for argument, upon great or petty subjects. He availed himself of every opportunity to speak. "During five whole sessions," he said, "I spoke every night but one; and I regret that I did not speak on that night, too."

Theodore Parker

Theodore Parker always read his sermons aloud while writing them, in order to test their "speaking quality." His opinion was that an impressive delivery depended particularly upon vigorous feeling, energetic thinking, and clearness of statement.

Henry Ward Beecher

Henry Ward Beecher's method was to practise vocal exercises in the open air, exploding all the vowel sounds in various keys. This practise duly produced a most flexible instrument, which served him throughout his brilliant career. He said:

"I had from childhood impediments of speech arising from a large palate, so that when a boy I used to be laughed at for talking as if I had a pudding in my mouth. When I went to Amherst, I was fortunate in passing into the hands of John Lovell, a teacher of elocution, and a better teacher for my purpose I can not conceive of. His system consisted in drill, or the thorough practise of inflections by the voice, of gesture, posture and articulation. Sometimes I was a whole hour practising my voice on a word—like justice. I would have to take a posture, frequently at a mark chalked on the floor.

Then we would go through all the gestures, exercising each movement of the arm and throwing open the hand. All gestures except those of precision go in curves, the arm rising from the side, coming to the front, turning to the left or right. I was drilled as to how far the arm should come forward, where it should start from, how far go back, and under what circumstances these movements should be made. It was drill, drill, drill, until the motions almost became a second nature. Now, I never know what movements I shall make. My gestures are natural, because this drill made them natural to me. The only method of acquiring effective elocution is by practise, of not less than an hour a day, until the student has his voice and himself thoroughly subdued and trained to get right expression."

Lord Bolingbroke

Lord Bolingbroke made it a rule always to speak well in daily conversation, however unimportant the occasion. His taste and accuracy at last gave him a style in ordinary speech worthy to have been put into print as it fell from his lips.

Lord Chatham

Lord Chatham, despite his great natural endowments for speaking, devoted a regular time each day to developing a varied and copious vocabulary. He twice examined each word in the dictionary, from beginning to end, in his ardent desire to master the English language.

John Philpot Curran

The well-known case of John Philpot Curran should give encouragement to every aspiring student of public speaking. He was generally known as "Orator

Mum," because of his failure in his first attempt at public speaking. But he resolved to develop his oratorical powers, and devoted every morning to intense reading. In addition, he regularly carried in his pocket a small copy of a classic for convenient reading at odd moments.

It is said that he daily practised declamation before a looking-glass, closely scrutinizing his gesture, posture, and manner. He was an earnest student of public speaking, and eventually became one of the most eloquent of world orators.

Balfour

Among present-day speakers in England Mr. Balfour occupies a leading place. He possesses the gift of never saying a word too much, a habit which might be copied to advantage by many public speakers. His habit during a debate is to scribble a few words on an envelop, and then to speak with rare facility of English style.

Bonar Law

Bonar Law does not use any notes in the preparation of a speech, but carefully thinks out the various parts, and then by means of a series of "mental rehearsals" fixes them indelibly in his mind. The result of this conscientious practise has made him a formidable debater and extempore speaker.

Asquith

Herbert H. Asquith, who possesses the rare gift of summoning the one inevitable word, and of compressing his speeches into a small space of time, speaks with equal success whether from a prepared manuscript or wholly extempore. His unsurpassed English style is the result of many years reading and study of prose masterpieces. "He produces, wherever and whenever he wants them, an endless succession of perfectly coined sentences, conceived with unmatched felicity and delivered without hesitation in a parliamentary style which is at once the envy and the despair of imitators."

Bryan

William Jennings Bryan is by common consent one of the greatest public speakers in America. He has a voice of unusual power and compass, and his delivery is natural and deliberate. His style is generally forensic, altho he frequently rises to the dramatic. He has been a diligent student of oratory, and once said:

"The age of oratory has not passed; nor will it pass. The press, instead of displacing the orator, has given him a larger audience and enabled him to do a more extended work. As long as there are human rights to be defended; as long as there are great interests to be guarded; as long as the welfare of nations is a matter for discussion, so long will public speaking have its place."

Roosevelt

Theodore Roosevelt was one of the most effective of American public speakers, due in large measure to intense moral earnestness and great stores of physical vitality. His diction was direct and his style energetic. He spoke out of the fulness of a well-furnished mind.

SUCCESS FACTORS IN PLATFORM SPEAKING

Constant practise of composition has been the habit of all great orators. This, combined with the habit of reading and re-reading the best prose writers and poets, accounts in large measure for the felicitous style of such men as Burke, Erskine, Macaulay, Bolingbroke, Phillips, Everett and Webster.

I can not too often urge you to use your pen in daily composition as a means to felicity and facility of speech. The act of writing out your thoughts is a direct aid to concentration, and tends to enforce the habit of choosing the best language. It gives clearness, force, precision, beauty, and copiousness of style, so valuable in extemporaneous and impromptu speaking.

Advantages and Disadvantages of Memorizing Speeches

Some of the most highly successful speakers carefully wrote out, revised, and committed to memory important passages in their speeches. These they dexterously wove into the body of their addresses in such a natural manner as not to expose their method.

This plan, however, is not to be generally recommended, since few men have the faculty of rendering memorized parts so as to make them appear extempore. If you recite rather than speak to an audience, you may be a good entertainer, but just to that degree will you impair your power and effectiveness as a public speaker.

There are speakers who have successfully used the plan of committing to memory significant sentences, statements, or sayings, and skilfully embodying them in their speeches. You might test this method for yourself, tho it is attended with danger.

If possible, join a local debating society, where you will have excellent opportunity for practise in thinking and speaking on your feet. Many distinguished public speakers have owed their fluency of speech and self-confidence to early practise in debate.

The Value of Repetition

Persuasion is a task of skill. You must bring to your aid in speaking every available resource. An effective weapon at times is a "remorseless iteration." Have the courage to repeat yourself as often as may be necessary to impress your leading ideas upon the minds of your hearers. Note the forensic maxim, "tell a judge twice whatever you want him to hear; tell a special jury thrice, and a common jury half a dozen times, the view of a case you wish them to entertain."

The Need of Self-Confidence

Whatever methods of premeditation you adopt in the preparation of a speech, having planned everything to the best of your ability, dismiss from your mind all anxiety and all thought about yourself.

Right preparation and earnest practise should give you a full degree of confidence in your ability to perform the task before you. When you stand at last before the audience, it should be with the assurance that you are thoroughly equipped to say something of real interest and importance.

The Power of Personality

Personality plays a vital part in a speaker's success. Gladstone described Cardinal Newman's manner in the pulpit as unsatisfactory if considered in its separate parts. "There was not much change in the inflection of his voice; action there was none; his sermons were read, and his eyes were always on his book; and all that, you will say, is against efficiency in preaching. Yes; but you take the man as a whole, and there was a stamp and a seal upon him, there was solemn music and sweetness in his tone, there was a completeness in the figure, taken together with the tone and with the manner, which made even his delivery such as I have described it, and tho exclusively with written sermons, singularly attractive."

The Danger of Imitation

It is a fatal mistake, as I have said, to set out deliberately to imitate some favorite speaker, and to mold your style after his. You will observe certain things and methods in other speakers which will fit in naturally with your style and temperament. To this extent you may advantageously adopt them, but always be on your guard against anything which might in the slightest degree impair your own individuality.

SPEECH FOR STUDY, WITH LESSON TALK

Features of an Eloquent Address

You will find useful material for study and practise in the speech which follows, delivered by Lord Rosebery at the Unveiling of the Statue of Gladstone at Glasgow, Scotland, October 11th, 1902.

The English style is noteworthy for its uniform charm and naturalness. There is an unmistakable personal note which contributes greatly to the effect of the speaker's words.

This eloquent address is a model for such an occasion, and a good illustration of the work of a speaker thoroughly familiar with his theme. It has sufficient variety to sustain interest, dignity in keeping with the subject, and a note of inspiration which would profoundly impress an audience of thinking men. It is a scholarly address.

Note the concise introductory sentences. Repeat them aloud and observe how easily they flow from the lips. Notice the balance and variety of successive sentences, the stately diction, and the underlying tone of deep sincerity.

Examine every phrase and sentence of this eloquent speech. Study the conclusion and particularly the closing paragraph. When you have thoroughly analyzed the speech, stand up and render it aloud in clear-cut tones and appropriately dignified style.

Speech for Study

At the Unveiling of the Statue of Gladstone

(Address of Lord Rosebery)

I am here to-day to unveil the image of one of the great figures of our country. It is right and fitting that it should stand here. A statue of Mr. Gladstone is congenial in any part of Scotland. But in this Scottish city, teeming with eager workers, endowed with a great University, a center of industry, commerce, and thought, a statue of William Ewart Gladstone is at home.

But you in Glasgow have more personal claims to a share in the inheritance of Mr. Gladstone's fame. I, at any rate, can recall one memory—the record of that marvelous day in December, 1879, nearly twenty-three years ago, when the indomitable old man delivered his rectorial address to the students at noon, a long political speech in St. Andrew's Hall in the evening, and a substantial discourse on receiving an address from the Corporation at ten o'clock at night. Some of you may have been present at all these gatherings, some only at the political meeting. If they were, they may remember the little incidents of the meeting—the glasses which were hopelessly lost and then, of course, found on the orator's person—the desperate candle brought in, stuck in a water-bottle, to attempt sufficient light to read an extract. And what a meeting it was—teeming, delirious, absorbed! Do you have such meetings now? They seem to me pretty good; but the meetings of that time stand out before all others in my mind.

This statue is erected, not out of the national subscription, but by the contributions from men of all creeds in Glasgow and in the West. I must then, in what I have to say, leave out altogether the political aspect of Mr. Gladstone. In some cases such a rule would omit all that was interesting in a man. There are characters, from which if you subtracted politics, there would be nothing left. It was not so with Mr. Gladstone.

To the great mass of his fellow-countrymen he was of course a statesman, wildly worshipped by some, wildly detested by others. But, to those who were privileged to know him, his politics seemed but the least part of him. The predominant part, to which all else was subordinated, was his religion; the life which seemed to attract him most was the life of the library; the subject which engrossed him most was the subject of the moment, whatever it might be, and that, when he was out of office, was very rarely politics. Indeed, I sometimes doubt whether his natural bent was toward politics at all. Had his course taken him that way, as it very nearly did, he would have been a great churchman, greater perhaps than any that this island has known; he would have been a great professor, if you could have found a university big enough to hold him; he would have been a great historian, a great bookman, he would have grappled with whole libraries and wrestled with academies, had the fates placed him in a cloister; indeed it is difficult to conceive the career, except perhaps the military, in which his energy and intellect and application would not have placed him on a summit. Politics, however, took him and claimed his life service, but, jealous mistress as she is, could never thoroughly absorb him.

Such powers as I have indicated seem to belong to a giant and a prodigy, and I can understand many turning away from the contemplation of such a character, feeling that it is too far removed from them to interest them, and that it is too unapproachable to help them—that it is like reading of Hercules or Hector, mythical heroes whose achievements the actual living mortal can not hope to rival. Well, that is true enough; we have not received intellectual faculties equal to Mr. Gladstone's, and can not hope to vie with him in their exercise. But apart from them, his great force was character, and amid the vast multitude that I am addressing, there is none who may not be helped by him.

The three signal qualities which made him what he was, were courage, industry, and faith; dauntless courage, unflagging industry, a faith which was part of his fiber; these were the levers with which he moved the world.

I do not speak of his religious faith, that demands a worthier speaker and another occasion. But no one who knew Mr. Gladstone could fail to see that it was the essence, the savor, the motive power of his life.

Strange as it may seem, I can not doubt that while this attracted many to him, it alienated others, others not themselves irreligious, but who suspected the sincerity of so manifest a devotion, and who, reared in the moderate atmosphere of the time, disliked the intrusion of religious considerations into politics. These, however, though numerous enough, were the exceptions, and it can not, I think, be questioned that Mr. Gladstone not merely raised the tone of public discussion, but quickened and renewed the religious feeling of the society in which he moved.

But this is not the faith of which I am thinking to-day. What is present to me is the faith with which he espoused and pursued great causes. There also he had faith sufficient to move mountains, and did sometimes move mountains. He did not lightly resolve, he came to no hasty conclusion, but when he had convinced himself that a cause was right, it engrossed him, it inspired him, with a certainty as deep-seated and as imperious as ever moved mortal man. To him, then, obstacles, objections, the counsels of doubters and critics were as nought, he pressed on with the passion of a whirlwind, but also with the steady persistence of some puissant machine.

He had, of course, like every statesman, often to traffic with expediency, he had always, I suppose, to accept something less than his ideal, but his unquenchable faith, not in himself—tho that with experience must have waxed strong—not in himself but in his cause, sustained him among the necessary shifts and transactions of the moment, and kept his head high in the heavens.

Such faith, such moral conviction, is not given to all men, for the treasures of his nature were in ingots, and not in dust. But there is, perhaps, no man without some faith in some cause or some person; if so, let him take heart, in however small a minority he may be, by remembering how mighty a strength was Gladstone's power of faith.

His next great force lay in his industry. I do not know if the aspersions of "ca' canny" be founded, but at any rate there was no "ca' canny" about him. From his earliest school-days, if tradition be true, to the bed of death, he gave his full time and energy to work. No doubt his capacity for labor was unusual. He would sit up all night writing a pamphlet, and work next day as usual. An eight-hours' day would have been a holiday to him, for he preached and practised the gospel of work to its fullest extent. He did not, indeed, disdain pleasure; no one enjoyed physical exercise, or a good play, or a pleasant dinner, more than he; he drank in deep draughts of the highest and the best that life had to offer; but even in pastime he was never idle. He did not know what it was to saunter, he debited himself with every minute of his time; he combined with the highest intellectual powers the faculty of utilizing them to the fullest extent by intense application. Moreover, his industry was prodigious in result, for he was an extraordinarily rapid worker. Dumont says of Mirabeau, that till he met that marvelous man he had no idea of how much could be achieved in a day. "Had I not lived with him," he says, "I should not know what can be accomplished in a day, all that can be comprest into an interval of twelve hours. A day was worth more to him than a week or a month to others." Many men can be busy for hours with a mighty small product, but with Mr. Gladstone every minute was fruitful. That, no doubt, was largely due to his marvelous powers of concentration. When he was staying at Dalmeny in 1879 he kindly consented to sit for his bust. The only difficulty was that there was no time for sittings. So the sculptor with his clay model was placed opposite Mr. Gladstone as he worked, and they spent the mornings together, Mr. Gladstone writing away, and the clay figure of himself less than a yard off gradually assuming shape and form. Anything more distracting I can not conceive, but it had no effect on the busy patient. And now let me make a short digression. I saw recently in your newspapers that there was some complaint of the manners of the rising generation in Glasgow. If that be so, they are heedless of Mr. Gladstone's example. It might be thought that so impetuous a temper as his might be occasionally rough or abrupt. That was not so. His exquisite urbanity was one of his most conspicuous graces. I do not now only allude to that grave, old-world courtesy, which gave so much distinction to his private life; for his sweetness of manner went far beyond demeanor. His spoken words, his letters, even when one differed from him most acutely, were all marked by this special note. He did not like people to disagree with him, few people do; but, so far as manner went, it was more pleasant to disagree with Mr. Gladstone than to be in agreement with some others.

Lastly, I come to his courage—that perhaps was his greatest quality, for when he gave his heart and reason to a cause, he never counted the cost. Most men are physically brave, and this nation is reputed to be especially brave, but Mr. Gladstone was brave among the brave. He had to the end the vitality of physical courage. When well on in his ninth decade, well on to ninety, he was knocked over by a cab, and before the bystanders could rally to his assistance, he had pursued the cab with a view to taking its number. He had, too, notoriously, political courage in a not less degree than Sir Robert Walpole. We read that George II, who was little given to enthusiasm, would often cry out, with color flushing into his cheeks, and tears sometimes in his eyes, and with a vehement oath:—"He (Walpole) is a brave fellow; he has more spirit than any man I ever knew."

Mr. Gladstone did not yield to Walpole in political and parliamentary courage—it was a quality which he closely observed in others, and on which he was fond of descanting. But he had the rarest and choicest courage of all—I mean moral courage. That was his supreme characteristic, and it was with him, like others, from the first. A contemporary of his at Eton once told me of a scene, at which my informant was present, when some loose or indelicate toast was proposed, and all present drank it but young Gladstone. In spite of the storm of objurgation and ridicule that raged around him, he jammed his face, as it were, down in his hands on the table and would not budge. Every schoolboy knows, for we may here accurately use Macaulay's well-known expression, every schoolboy knows the courage that this implies. And even by the heedless generation of boyhood it was appreciated, for we find an Etonian writing to his parents to ask that he might go to Oxford rather than Cambridge, on the sole ground that at Oxford he would have the priceless advantage of Gladstone's influence and example. Nor did his courage ever flag. He might be right, or he might be wrong—that is not the question here—but when he was convinced that he was right, not all the combined powers of Parliament or society or the multitude could for an instant hinder his course, whether it ended in success or in failure. Success left him calm, he had had so much of it; nor did failures greatly depress him. The next morning found him once more facing the world with serene and undaunted brow. There was a man. The nation has lost him, but preserves his character, his manhood, as a model, on which she may form if she be fortunate, coming generations of men. With his politics, with his theology, with his manifold graces and gifts of intellect, we are not concerned to-day, not even with his warm and passionate human sympathies. They are not dead with him, but let them rest with him, for we can not in one discourse view him in all his parts. To-day it is enough to have dealt for a moment on three of his great moral characteristics, enough to have snatched from the fleeting hour a few moments of communion with the mighty dead.

History has not yet allotted him his definite place, but no one would now deny that he bequeathed a pure standard of life, a record of lofty ambition for the public good as he understood it, a monument of life-long labor. Such lives speak for themselves, they need no statues, they face the future with the confidence of high purpose and endeavor. The statues are not for them but for us, to bid us be conscious of our trust, mindful of our duty, scornful of opposition to principle and faith. They summon us to account for time and opportunity, they embody an inspiring tradition, they are milestones in the life of a nation. The effigy of Pompey was bathed in the blood of his great rival: let this statue have the nobler destiny of constantly calling to life worthy rivals of Gladstone's fame and character.

Unveil, then, that statue. Let it stand to Glasgow in all time coming for faith, fortitude, courage, industry, qualities apart from intellect or power or wealth, which may inspire all her citizens however humble, however weak; let it remind the most unthinking passer-by of the dauntless character which it represents, of his long life and honest purpose; let it leaven by an immortal tradition the population which lives and works and dies around this monument.

Study of Model Speeches

Model Speeches, with Suggestions
For Their Study

There is no better way for you to improve your own public speaking than to analyze and study the speeches of successful orators.

First read such speeches aloud, since by that means you fit words to your lips and acquire a familiarity with oratorical style.

Then examine the speaker's method of arranging his thoughts, and the precise way in which they lead up and contribute to his ultimate object.

Carefully note any special means employed—story, illustration, appeal, or climax,—to increase the effectiveness of the speech.

John Stuart Mill

Read the following speech delivered by John Stuart Mill, in his tribute to Garrison. Note the clear-cut English of the speaker. Observe how promptly he goes to his subject, and how steadily he keeps to it. Particularly note the high level of thought maintained throughout. This is an excellent model of dignified, well-reasoned, convincing speech.

"Mr. Chairman, Ladies, and Gentlemen,—The speakers who have preceded me have, with an eloquence far beyond anything which I can command, laid before our honored guest the homage of admiration and gratitude which we all feel due to his heroic life. Instead of idly expatiating upon things which have been far better said than I could say them, I would rather endeavor to recall one or two lessons applicable to ourselves, which may be drawn from his career. A noble work nobly done always contains in itself not one but many lessons; and in the case of him whose character and deeds we are here to commemorate, two may be singled out specially deserving to be laid to heart by all who would wish to leave the world better than they found it.

"The first lesson is,—Aim at something great; aim at things which are difficult; and there is no great thing which is not difficult. Do not pare down your undertaking to what you can hope to see successful in the next few years, or in the years of your own life. Fear not the reproach of Quixotism or of fanaticism; but after you have well weighed what you undertake, if you see your way clearly, and are convinced that you are right, go forward, even tho you, like Mr. Garrison, do it at the risk of being torn to pieces by the very men through whose changed hearts your purpose will one day be accomplished. Fight on with all your strength against whatever odds and with however small a band of supporters. If you are right, the time will come when that small band will swell into a multitude; you will at least lay the foundations of something memorable, and you may, like Mr. Garrison—tho you ought not to need or expect so great a reward—be spared to see that work completed which, when you began it, you only hoped it might be given to you to help forward a few stages on its way.

"The other lesson which it appears to me important to enforce, amongst the many that may be drawn from our friend's life, is this: If you aim at something noble and succeed in it, you will generally find that you have succeeded not in that alone. A hundred other good and noble things which you never dreamed of will have been accomplished by the way, and the more certainly, the sharper and more agonizing has been the struggle which preceded the victory. The heart and mind of a nation are never stirred from their foundations without manifold good fruits. In the case of the great American contest these fruits have been already great, and are daily becoming greater. The prejudices which beset every form of society—and of which there was a plentiful crop in America—are rapidly melting away. The chains of prescription have been broken; it is not only the slave who has been freed—the mind of America has been emancipated. The whole intellect of the country has been set thinking about the fundamental questions of society and government; and the new problems which have to be solved and the new difficulties which have to be encountered are calling forth new activity of thought, and that great nation is saved probably for a long time to come, from the most formidable danger of a completely settled state of society and opinion—intellectual and moral stagnation. This, then, is an additional item of the debt which America and mankind owe to Mr. Garrison and his noble associates; and it is well calculated to deepen our sense of the truth which his whole career most strikingly illustrates—that tho our best directed efforts may often seem wasted and lost, nothing coming of them that can be pointed to and distinctly identified as a definite gain to humanity, tho this may happen ninety-nine times in every hundred, the hundredth time the result may be so great and dazzling that we had never dared to hope for it, and should have regarded him who had predicted it to us as sanguine beyond the bounds of mental sanity. So has it been with Mr. Garrison."

It will be beneficial for your all-round development in speaking to choose for earnest study several speeches of widely different character. As you compare one speech with another, you will more readily see why each subject requires a different form of treatment, and also learn to judge how the speaker has availed himself of the possibilities afforded him.

Judge Story

The speech which follows is a fine example of elevated and impassioned oratory. Judge Story here lauds the American Republic, and employs to advantage the rhetorical figures of exclamation and interrogation.

As you examine this speech you will notice that the speaker himself was moved by deep conviction. His own belief stamped itself upon his words, and throughout there is the unmistakable mark of sincerity.

You are impressed by the comprehensive treatment of the subject. The orator here speaks out of a full mind, and you feel that you would confidently trust yourself to his leadership.

"When we reflect on what has been and what is, how is it possible not to feel a profound sense of the responsibilities of this Republic to all future ages? What vast motives press upon us for lofty efforts! What brilliant prospects invite our enthusiasm! What solemn warnings at once demand our vigilance and moderate our confidence! The Old World has already revealed to us, in its unsealed books, the beginning and the end of all marvelous struggles in the cause of liberty.

"Greece! lovely Greece! 'the land of scholars and the nurse of arms,' where sister republics, in fair processions chanted the praise of liberty and the good, where and what is she? For two thousand years the oppressors have bound her to the earth. Her arts are no more. The last sad relics of her temples are but the barracks of a ruthless soldiery; the fragments of her columns and her palaces are in the dust, yet beautiful in ruins.

"She fell not when the mighty were upon her. Her sons united at Thermopylæ and Marathon; and the tide of her triumph rolled back upon the Hellespont. She was conquered by her own factions—she fell by the hands of her own people. The man of Macedonia did not the work of destruction. It was already done by her own corruptions, banishments, and dissensions. Rome! whose eagles glanced in the rising and setting sun, where and what is she! The Eternal City yet remains, proud even in her desolation, noble in her decline, venerable in the majesty of religion, and calm as in the composure of death.

"The malaria has but traveled in the parts won by the destroyers. More than eighteen centuries have mourned over the loss of the empire. A mortal disease was upon her before Cæsar had crossed the Rubicon; and Brutus did not restore her health by the deep probings of the senate-chamber. The Goths, and Vandals, and Huns, the swarms of the North, completed only what was begun at home. Romans betrayed Rome. The legions were bought and sold, but the people offered the tribute-money.

"And where are the republics of modern times, which cluster around immortal Italy? Venice and Genoa exist but in name. The Alps, indeed, look down upon the brave and peaceful Swiss in their native fastnesses;

but the guaranty of their freedom is in their weakness, and not in their strength. The mountains are not easily crossed, and the valleys are not easily retained.

"When the invader comes, he moves like an avalanche, carrying destruction in his path. The peasantry sink before him. The country, too, is too poor for plunder, and too rough for a valuable conquest. Nature presents her eternal barrier on every side, to check the wantonness of ambition. And Switzerland remains with her simple institutions, a military road to climates scarcely worth a permanent possession, and protected by the jealousy of her neighbors.

"We stand the latest, and if we fall, probably the last experiment of self-government by the people. We have begun it under circumstances of the most auspicious nature. We are in the vigor of youth. Our growth has never been checked by the oppression of tyranny. Our Constitutions never have been enfeebled by the vice or the luxuries of the world. Such as we are, we have been from the beginning: simple, hardy, intelligent, accustomed to self-government and self-respect.

"The Atlantic rolls between us and a formidable foe. Within our own territory, stretching through many degrees of latitude, we have the choice of many products, and many means of independence. The government is mild. The press is free. Religion is free. Knowledge reaches, or may reach every home. What fairer prospects of success could be presented? What means more adequate to accomplish the sublime end? What more is necessary than for the people to preserve what they themselves have created?

"Already has the age caught the spirit of our institutions. It has already ascended the Andes, and snuffed the breezes of both oceans. It has infused itself into the life-blood of Europe, and warmed the sunny plains of France and the lowlands of Holland. It has touched the philosophy of Germany and the North, and, moving onward to the South, has opened to Greece the lesson of her better days.

"Can it be that America under such circumstances should betray herself? That she is to be added to the catalog of republics, the inscription upon whose ruin is, 'They were but they are not!' Forbid it, my countrymen! forbid it, Heaven! I call upon you, fathers, by the shades of your ancestors, by the dear ashes which repose in this precious soil, by all you are, and all you hope to be, resist every attempt to fetter your consciences, or smother your public schools, or extinguish your system of public instruction.

"I call upon you, mothers, by that which never fails in woman, the love of your offspring, to teach them as they climb your knees or lean on your bosoms, the blessings of liberty. Swear them at the altar, as with their baptismal vows, to be true to their country, and never forsake her. I call upon you, young men, to remember whose sons you are—whose inheritance you possess. Life can never be too short, which brings nothing but disgrace and oppression. Death never comes too soon, if necessary, in defense of the liberties of our country."

You can advantageously read aloud many times a speech like the foregoing. Stand up and read it aloud once a day for a month, and you will be conscious of a distinct improvement in your own command of persuasive speech.

W. J. Fox

The following is a specimen of masterly oratorical style, from a sermon preached in London, England, by W. J. Fox:

"From the dawn of intellect and freedom Greece has been a watchword on the earth. There rose the social spirit to soften and refine her chosen race, and shelter as in a nest her gentleness from the rushing storm of barbarism; there liberty first built her mountain throne, first called the waves her own, and shouted across them a proud defiance to despotism's banded myriads, there the arts and graces danced around humanity, and stored man's home with comforts, and strewed his path with roses, and bound his brows with myrtle, and fashioned for him the breathing statue, and summoned him to temples of snowy marble, and charmed his senses with all forms of eloquence, and threw over his final sleep their veil of loveliness; there sprung poetry, like their own fabled goddess, mature at once from the teeming intellect, gilt with arts and armour that defy the assaults of time and subdue the heart of man; there matchless orators gave the world a model of perfect eloquence, the soul the instrument on which they played, and every passion of our nature but a tone which the master's touch called forth at will; there lived and taught the philosophers of bower and porch, of pride and pleasure, of deep speculation, and of useful action, who developed all the acuteness and refinement, and excursiveness, and energy of mind, and were the glory of their country when their country was the glory of the earth."

William McKinley

An eloquent speech, worthy of close study, is that of William McKinley on "The Characteristics of Washington." As you read it aloud, note the short, clear-cut sentences used in the introduction. Observe how the long sentence at the third paragraph gives the needed variation. Carefully study the compact English style, and the use of forceful expressions of the speaker, as "He blazed the path to liberty."

"Fellow Citizens:—There is a peculiar and tender sentiment connected with this memorial. It expresses not only the gratitude and reverence of the living, but is a testimonial of affection and homage from the dead.

"The comrades of Washington projected this monument. Their love inspired it. Their contributions helped to build it. Past and present share in its completion, and future generations will profit by its lessons. To participate in the dedication of such a monument is a rare and precious privilege. Every monument to Washington is a tribute to patriotism. Every shaft and statue to his memory helps to inculcate love of country, encourage loyalty, and establish a better citizenship. God bless every undertaking which revives patriotism and rebukes the indifferent and lawless! A critical study of Washington's career only enhances our estimation of his vast and varied abilities.

"As Commander-in-chief of the Colonial armies from the beginning of the war to the proclamation of peace, as president of the convention which framed the Constitution of the United States, and as the first President of the United States under that Constitution, Washington has a distinction differing from that of all other illustrious Americans. No other name bears or can bear such a relation to the Government. Not only by his military genius—his patience, his sagacity, his courage, and his skill—was our national independence won, but he helped in largest measure to draft the chart by which the Nation was guided; and he was the first chosen of the people to put in motion the new Government. His was not the boldness of martial display or the charm of captivating oratory, but his calm and steady judgment won men's support and commanded their confidence by appealing to their best and noblest aspirations. And withal Washington was ever so modest that at no time in his career did his personality seem in the least intrusive. He was above the temptation of power. He spurned the suggested crown. He would have no honor which the people did not bestow.

"An interesting fact—and one which I love to recall—is that the only time Washington formally addrest the Constitutional Convention during all its sessions over which he presided in this city, he appealed for a larger representation of the people in the National House of Representatives, and his appeal was instantly heeded. Thus was he ever keenly watchful of the rights of the people in whose hands was the destiny of our Government then as now.

"Masterful as were his military campaigns, his civil administration commands equal admiration. His foresight was marvelous; his conception of the philosophy of government, his insistence upon the necessity of education, morality, and enlightened citizenship to the progress and permanence of the Republic can not be contemplated even at this period without filling us with astonishment at the breadth of his comprehension and the sweep of his vision. His was no narrow view of government. The immediate present was not the sole concern, but our future good his constant theme of study. He blazed the path of liberty. He laid the foundation upon which we have grown from weak and scattered Colonial governments to a united Republic whose domains and power as well as whose liberty and freedom have become the admiration of the world. Distance and time have not detracted from the fame and force of his achievements or diminished the grandeur of his life and work. Great deeds do not stop in their growth, and those of Washington will expand in influence in all the centuries to follow.

"The bequest Washington has made to civilization is rich beyond computation. The obligations under which he has placed mankind are sacred and commanding. The responsibility he has left, for the American people to preserve and perfect what he accomplished, is exacting and solemn. Let us rejoice in every new evidence that the people realize what they enjoy, and cherish with affection the illustrious heroes of Revolutionary story whose valor and sacrifices made us a nation. They live in us, and their memory will help us keep the covenant entered into for the maintenance of the freest Government of earth.

"The nation and the name Washington are inseparable. One is linked indissolubly with the other. Both are glorious, both triumphant. Washington lives and will live because of what he did for the exaltation of man, the enthronement of conscience, and the establishment of a Government which recognizes all the governed. And so, too, will the Nation live victorious over all obstacles, adhering to the immortal principles which Washington taught and Lincoln sustained."

Edward Everett

The following extract from "The Foundation of National Character," by Edward Everett, is a fine example of patriotic appeal. Read it aloud, and note how the orator speaks with deep feeling and stirs the same feeling in you. This impression is largely due to the simple, sincere, right-onward style of the speaker,—qualities of his own well-known character.

It will amply repay you to read this extract aloud at least once a day for a week or more, so that its superior elements of thought and style may be deeply imprest on your mind.

"How is the spirit of a free people to be formed, and animated, and cheered, but out of the storehouse of its historic recollections? Are we to be eternally ringing the changes upon Marathon and Thermopylæ; and going back to read in obscure texts of Greek and Latin, of the exemplars of patriotic virtue?

"I thank God that we can find them nearer home, in our own soil; that strains of the noblest sentiment that ever swelled in the breast of man, are breathing to us out of every page of our country's history, in the native eloquence of our mother-tongue,—that the colonial and provincial councils of America exhibit to us models of the spirits and character which gave Greece and Rome their name and their praise among nations.

"Here we ought to go for our instruction;—the lesson is plain, it is clear, it is applicable. When we go to ancient history, we are bewildered with the difference of manners and institutions. We are willing to pay our tribute of applause to the memory of Leonidas, who fell nobly for his country in the face of his foe.

"But when we trace him to his home, we are confounded at the reflection, that the same Spartan heroism, to which he sacrificed himself at Thermopylæ, would have led him to tear his own child, if it had happened to be a sickly babe,—the very object for which all that is kind and good in man rises up to plead,—from the bosom of his mother, and carry it out to be eaten by the wolves of Taygetus.

"We feel a glow of admiration at the heroism displayed at Marathon by the ten thousand champions of invaded Greece; but we can not forget that the tenth part of the number were slaves, unchained from the workshops and doorposts of their masters, to go and fight the battles of freedom.

"I do not mean that these examples are to destroy the interest with which we read the history of ancient times; they possibly increase that interest by the very contrast they exhibit. But they warn us, if we need the warning, to seek our great practical lessons of patriotism at home; out of the exploits and sacrifices of which our own country is the theater; out of the characters of our own fathers.

"Them we know,—the high-souled, natural, unaffected, the citizen heroes. We know what happy firesides they left for the cheerless camp. We know with what pacific habits they dared the perils of the field. There is no mystery, no romance, no madness, under the name of chivalry about them. It is all resolute, manly resistance for conscience and liberty's sake not merely of an overwhelming power, but of all the force of long-rooted habits and native love of order and peace.

"Above all, their blood calls to us from the soil which we tread; it beats in our veins; it cries to us not merely in the thrilling words of one of the first victims in this cause—'My sons, scorn to be slaves!'—but it cries with a still more moving eloquence—'My sons, forget not your fathers!'"

John Quincy Adams

John Quincy Adams, in his speech on "The Life and Character of Lafayette," gives us a fine example of elevated and serious-minded utterance. The following extract from this speech can be studied with profit. Particularly note the use of sustained sentences, and the happy collocation of words. The concluding paragraph should be closely examined as a study in impressive climax.

"Pronounce him one of the first men of his age, and you have yet not done him justice. Try him by that test to which he sought in vain to stimulate the vulgar and selfish spirit of Napoleon; class him among the men who, to compare and seat themselves, must take in the compass of all ages; turn back your eyes upon the records of time; summon, from the creation of the world to this day, the mighty dead of every age and every clime,—and where, among the race of merely mortal men, shall one be found who, as the benefactor of his kind, shall claim to take precedence of Lafayette?

"There have doubtless been in all ages men whose discoveries or inventions in the world of matter, or of mind, have opened new avenues to the dominion of man over the material creation; have increased his means or his faculties of enjoyment; have raised him in nearer approximation to that higher and happier condition, the object of his hopes and aspirations in his present state of existence.

"Lafayette discovered no new principle of politics or of morals. He invented nothing in science. He disclosed no new phenomenon in the laws of nature. Born and educated in the highest order of feudal nobility, under the most absolute monarchy of Europe; in possession of an affluent fortune, and master of himself and of all his capabilities, at the moment of attaining manhood the principle of republican justice and of social equality took possession of his heart and mind, as if by inspiration from above.

"He devoted himself, his life, his fortune, his hereditary honors, his towering ambition, his splendid hopes, all to the cause of Liberty. He came to another hemisphere to defend her. He became one of the most effective champions of our independence; but, that once achieved, he returned to his own country, and thenceforward took no part in the controversies which have divided us.

"In the events of our Revolution, and in the forms of policy which we have adopted for the establishment and perpetuation of our freedom, Lafayette found the most perfect form of government. He wished to add nothing to it. He would gladly have abstracted nothing from it. Instead of the imaginary Republic of Plato, or the Utopia of Sir Thomas More, he took a practical existing model in actual operation here, and never attempted or wished more than to apply it faithfully to his own country.

"It was not given to Moses to enter the promised land; but he saw it from the summit of Pisgah. It was not given to Lafayette to witness the consummation of his wishes in the establishment of a Republic and the extinction of all hereditary rule in France. His principles were in advance of the age and hemisphere in which he lived.... The prejudices and passions of the people of France rejected the principle of inherited power in every station of public trust, excepting the first and highest of them all; but there they clung to it, as did the Israelites of old to the savory deities of Egypt.

"When the principle of hereditary dominion shall be extinguished in all the institutions of France; when government shall no longer be considered as property transmissible from sire to son, but as a trust committed for a limited time, and then to return to the people whence it came; as a burdensome duty to be discharged, and not as a reward to be abused;—then will be the time for contemplating the character of Lafayette, not merely in the events of his life, but in the full development of his intellectual conceptions, of his fervent aspirations, of the labors, and perils, and sacrifices of his long and eventful career upon earth; and thenceforward till the hour when the trumpet of the Archangel shall sound to announce that time shall be no more, the name of Lafayette shall stand enrolled upon the annals of our race high on the list of pure and disinterested benefactors of mankind."

I have selected these extracts for your convenient use, as embodying both thought and style worthy of your careful study. Read them aloud at every opportunity, and you will be gratified at the steady improvement such practise will make in your own speaking power.

HISTORY OF PUBLIC SPEAKING

Men Who have Made History in Public Speaking—and Their Methods

The great orators of the world did not regard eloquence as simply an endowment of nature, but applied themselves diligently to cultivating their powers of expression. In many cases there was unusual natural ability, but such men knew that regular study and practise were essential to success in this coveted art.

The oration can be traced back to Hebrew literature. In the first chapter of Deuteronomy we find Moses' speech in the end of the fortieth year, briefly rehearsing the story of God's promise, and of God's anger for their incredulity and disobedience.

The four orations in Deuteronomy, by Moses, are highly commended for their tenderness, sublimity and passionate appeal. You can advantageously read them aloud.

The oration of Pericles over the graves of those who fell in the Peloponnesian War, is said to have been the first Athenian oration designed for the public.

The agitated political times and the people's intense desire for learning combined to favor the development of oratory in ancient Greece. Questions of great moment had to be discust and serious problems solved. As the orator gradually became the most powerful influence in the State, the art of oratory was more and more recognized as the supreme accomplishment of the educated man.

Demosthenes

Demosthenes stands preeminent among Greek orators. His well-known oration "On the Crown," the preparation of which occupied a large part of seven years, is regarded as the oratorical masterpiece of all history.

It is encouraging to the student of public speaking to recall that this distinguished orator at first had serious natural defects to overcome. His voice was weak, he stammered in his speech, and was painfully diffident. These faults were remedied, as is well-known, by earnest daily practise in declaiming on the sea-shore, with pebbles in the mouth, walking up and down hill while reciting, and deliberately seeking occasions for conversing with groups of people.

The chief lesson for you to draw from Demosthenes is that he was indefatigable in his study of the art of oratory. He left nothing to chance. His speeches were characterized by deliberate forethought. He excelled other men not because of great natural ability but because of intelligent and continuous industry. He stands for all time as the most inspiring example of oratorical achievement, despite almost insuperable difficulties.

Cicero

The fame of Roman oratory rests upon Cicero, whose eloquence was second only to that of Demosthenes. He was a close student of the art of speaking. He was so intense and vehement by nature that he was obliged in his early career to spend two years in Greece, exercising in the gymnasium in order to restore his shattered constitution.

His nervous temperament clung to him, however, since he made this significant confession after long years of practise in public speaking. "I declare that when I think of the moment when I shall have to rise and speak in defense of a client, I am not only disturbed in mind, but tremble in every limb of my body."

It is well to note here that a nervous temperament may be a help rather than a hindrance to a speaker. Indeed, it is the highly sensitive nature that often produces the most persuasive orator, but only when he has learned to conserve and properly use this valuable power.

Cicero was a living embodiment of the comprehensive requirements laid down by the ancients as essential to the orator. He had a knowledge of logic, ethics, astronomy, philosophy, geometry, music, and rhetoric. Little wonder, therefore, that his amazing eloquence was described as a resistless torrent.

Luther

Martin Luther was the dominating orator of the Reformation. He combined a strong physique with great intellectual power. "If I wish to compose, or write, or pray, or preach well," said he, "I must be angry. Then all the blood in my veins is stirred, my understanding is sharpened, and all dismal thoughts and temptations are dissipated." What the great Reformer called "anger," we would call indignation or earnestness.

John Knox

John Knox, the Scotch reformer, was a preeminent preacher. His pulpit style was characterized by a fiery eloquence which stirred his hearers to great enthusiasm and sometimes to violence.

Bossuet

Bossuet, regarded as the greatest orator France has produced, was a fearless and inspired speaker. His style was dignified and deliberate, but as he warmed with his theme his thought took fire and he carried his hearers along upon a swiftly moving tide of impassioned eloquence. When he spoke from the text, "Be wise, therefore, O ye Kings! be instructed, ye judges of the earth!" the King himself was thrilled as with a religious terror.

To ripe scholarship Bossuet added a voice that was deep and sonorous, an imposing personality, and an animated style of gesture. Lamartine described his voice as "like that of the thunder in the clouds, or the organ in the cathedral."

Bourdaloue

Louis Bourdaloue, styled "the preacher of Kings, and the King of preachers," was a speaker of versatile powers. He could adapt his style to any audience, and "mechanics left their shops, merchants their business, and lawyers their court house" in order to hear him. His high personal character, simplicity of life, and clear and logical utterance combined to make him an accomplished orator.

Massillon

Massillon preached directly to the hearts of his hearers. He was of a deeply affectionate nature, hence his style was that of tender persuasiveness rather than of declamation. He had remarkable spiritual insight and knowledge of the human heart, and was himself deeply moved by the truths which he proclaimed to other men.

Lord Chatham

Lord Chatham's oratorical style was formed on the classic model. His intellect, at once comprehensive and vigorous, combined with deep and intense feeling, fitted him to become one of the highest types of orators. He was dignified and graceful, sometimes vehement, always commanding. He ruled the British parliament by sheer force of eloquence.

His voice was a wonderful instrument, so completely under control that his lowest whisper was distinctly heard, and his full tones completely filled the House. He had supreme self-confidence, and a sense of superiority over those around him which acted as an inspiration to his own mind.

Burke

Burke was a great master of English prose as well as a great orator. He took large means to deal with large subjects. He was a man of immense power, and his stride was the stride of a giant. He has been credited with passion, intensity, imagination, nobility, and amplitude. His style was sonorous and majestic.

Sheridan

Sheridan became a foremost parliamentary speaker and debater, despite early discouragements. His well-known answer to a friend, who adversely criticized his speaking, "It is in me, and it shall come out of me!" has for years given new encouragement to many a student of public speaking. He applied himself with untiring industry to the development of all his powers, and so became one of the most distinguished speakers of his day.

Charles James Fox

Charles James Fox was a plain, practical, forceful orator of the thoroughly English type. His qualities of sincerity, vehemence, simplicity, ruggedness, directness and dexterity, combined with a manly fearlessness, made him a formidable antagonist in any debate. Facts, analogies, illustrations, intermingled with wit, feeling, and ridicule, gave charm and versatility to his speaking unsurpassed in his time.

Lord Brougham

Lord Brougham excelled in cogent, effective argument. His impassioned reasoning often made ordinary things interesting. He ingratiated himself by his wise and generous sentiments, and his uncompromising solicitude for his country.

He always succeeded in getting through his protracted and parenthetical sentences without confusion to his hearers or to himself. He could see from the beginning of a sentence precisely what the end would be.

John Quincy Adams

John Quincy Adams won a high place as a debater and orator in his speech in Congress upon the right of petition, delivered in 1837. A formidable antagonist, pugnacious by temperament, uniformly dignified, a profound scholar,—his is "a name recorded on the brightest page of American history, as statesman, diplomatist, philosopher, orator, author, and, above all a Christian."

Patrick Henry

Patrick Henry was a man of extraordinary eloquence. In his day he was regarded as the greatest orator in America. In his early efforts as a speaker he hesitated much and throughout his career often gave an impression of natural timidity. He has been favorably compared with Lord Chatham for fire, force, and personal energy. His power was largely due to a rare gift of lucid and concise statement.

Henry Clay

The eloquence of Henry Clay was magisterial, persuasive, and irresistible. So great was his personal magnetism that multitudes came great distances to hear him. He was a man of brilliant intellect, fertile fancy, chivalrous nature, and patriotic fervor. He had a clear, rotund, melodious voice, under complete command. He held, it is said, the keys to the hearts of his countrymen.

Calhoun

The eloquence of John Caldwell Calhoun has been described by Daniel Webster as "plain, strong, terse, condensed, concise; sometimes impassioned, still always severe. Rejecting ornament, not often seeking far for illustrations, his power consisted in the plainness of his propositions, in the closeness of his logic, and in the earnestness and energy of his manner."

He exerted unusual influence over the opinions of great masses of men. He had remarkable power of analysis and logical skill. Originality, self-reliance, impatience, aggressiveness, persistence, sincerity, honesty, ardor,— these were some of the personal qualities which gave him dominating influence over his generation.

Daniel Webster

Daniel Webster was a massive orator. He combined logical and argumentative skill with a personality of extraordinary power and attractiveness. He had a su-

preme scorn for tricks of oratory, and a horror of epi-
thets and personalities. His best known speeches are
those delivered on the anniversary at Plymouth, the
laying of the corner-stone of Bunker Hill monument,
and the deaths of Jefferson and Adams.

Edward Everett

Edward Everett was a man of scholastic tastes and
habits. His speaking style was remarkable for its liter-
ary finish and polished precision. His sense of fitness
saved him from serious faults of speech or manner. He
blended many graces in one, and his speeches are worthy of study as models of oratorical style.

Rufus Choate

Rufus Choate was a brilliant and persuasive extempore
speaker. He possest in high degree faculties essential
to great oratory—a capacious mind, retentive memory,
logical acumen, vivid imagination, deep concentration,
and wealth of language. He had an extraordinary personal fascination, largely due to his broad sympathy
and geniality.

Charles Sumner

Charles Sumner was a gifted orator. His delivery was
highly impressive, due fundamentally to his innate in-
tegrity and elevated personal character. He was a wide
reader and profound student. His style was energetic,
logical, and versatile. His intense patriotism and argumentative power, won large favor with his hearers.

William E. Channing

William Ellery Channing was a preacher of unusual
eloquence and intellectual power. He was small in
stature, but of surpassing grace. His voice was soft and

musical, and wonderfully responsive to every change of emotion that arose in his mind. His eloquence was not forceful nor forensic, but gentle and persuasive.

His monument bears this high tribute: "In memory of William Ellery Channing, honored throughout Christendom for his eloquence and courage in maintaining and advancing the great cause of truth, religion, and human freedom."

Wendell Phillips

Wendell Phillips was one of the most graceful and polished orators. To his conversational style he added an exceptional vocabulary, a clear and flexible voice, and a most fascinating personality.

He produced his greatest effects by the simplest means. He combined humor, pathos, sarcasm and invective with rare skill, yet his style was so simple that a child could have understood him.

George William Curtis

George William Curtis has been described in his private capacity as natural, gentle, manly, refined, simple, and unpretending. He was the last of the great school of Everett, Sumner, and Phillips.

His art of speaking had an enduring charm, and he completely satisfied the taste for pure and dignified speech. His voice was of silvery clearness, which carried to the furthermost part of the largest hall.

Gladstone

Gladstone was an orator of preeminent power. In fertility of thought, spontaneity of expression, modulation of voice, and grace of gesture, he has had few equals.

He always spoke from a deep sense of duty. When he began a sentence you could not always foresee how he would end it, but he always succeeded. He had an extraordinary wealth of words and command of the English language.

Gladstone has been described as having eagerness, self-control, mastery of words, gentle persuasiveness, prodigious activity, capacity for work, extreme seriousness, range of experience, constructive power, mastery of detail, and deep concentration. "So vast and so well ordered was the arsenal of his mind, that he could both instruct and persuade, stimulate his friends and demolish his opponents, and do all these things at an hour's notice."

He was essentially a devout man, and unquestionably his spiritual character was the fundamental secret of his transcendent power. A keen observer thus describes him:

"While this great and famous figure was in the House of Commons, the House had eyes for no other person. His movements on the bench, restless and eager, his demeanor when on his legs, whether engaged in answering a simple question, expounding an intricate Bill, or thundering in vehement declamation, his dramatic gestures, his deep and rolling voice with its wide compass and marked northern accent, his flashing eye, his almost incredible command of ideas and words, made a combination of irresistible fascination and power."

John Bright

John Bright won a foremost place among British orators largely because of his power of clear statement and vivid description. His manner was at once ingratiating and commanding.

His way of putting things was so lucid and convincing that it was difficult to express the same ideas in any other words with equal force. One of the secrets of his success, it is said, was his command of colloquial simile, apposite stories, and ready wit.

Mr. Bright always had himself well in hand, yet his style at times was volcanic in its force and impetuosity. He would shut himself up for days preparatory to delivering a great speech, and tho he committed many passages to memory, his manner in speaking was entirely free from artifice.

Lincoln

Lincoln's power as a speaker was due to a combination of rugged gifts. Self-reliance, sympathy, honesty, penetration, broad-mindedness, modesty, and independence,—these were keynotes to his great character.

The Gettysburg speech of less than 300 words is regarded as the greatest short speech in history.

Lincoln's aim was always to say the most sensible thing in the clearest terms, and in the fewest possible words. His supreme respect for his hearers won their like respect for him.

There is a valuable suggestion for the student of public speaking in this description of Lincoln's boyhood: "Abe read diligently. He read every book he could lay his hands on, and when he came across a passage that struck him, he would write it down on boards if he had no paper, and keep it there until he did get paper. Then he would rewrite it, look at it, repeat it. He had a copy book, a kind of scrap-book, in which he put down all things, and thus preserved them."

Daniel O'Connell

Daniel O'Connell was one of the most popular orators of his day. He had a deep, sonorous, flexible voice, which he used to great advantage. He had a wonderful gift of touching the human heart, now melting his hearers by his pathos, then convulsing them with his quaint humor. He was attractive in manner, generous in feeling, spontaneous in expression, and free from rhetorical trickery.

As you read this brief sketch of some of the world's great orators, it should be inspiring to you as a student of public speaking to know something of their trials, difficulties, methods and triumphs. They have left great examples to be emulated, and to read about them and to study their methods is to follow somewhat in their footsteps.

Great speeches, like great pictures, are inspired by great subjects and great occasions. When a speaker is moved to vindicate the national honor, to speak in defense of human rights, or in some other great cause, his thought and expression assume new and wonderful power. All the resources of his mind—will, imagination, memory, and emotion,—are stimulated into unusual activity. His theme takes complete possession of him and he carries conviction to his hearers by the force, sincerity, and earnestness of his delivery. It is to this exalted type of oratory I would have you aspire.

Extracts For Study, With Lesson Talk

Examples of Oratory and How to Study Them

It will be beneficial to you in this connection to study examples of speeches by the world's great orators. I furnish you here with a few short specimens which will serve this purpose. Carefully note the suggestions and the numbered extract to which they refer.

1. Practise this example for climax. As you read it aloud, gradually increase the intensity of your voice but do not unduly elevate the key.

2. Study this particularly for its suggestive value to you as a public speaker.

3. Practise this for fervent appeal. Articulate distinctly. Pause after each question. Do not rant or declaim, but speak it.

4. Study this for its sustained sentences and dignity of style.

5. Analyze this for its strength of thought and diction. Note the effective repetition of "I care not." Commit the passage to memory.

6. Read this for elevated and patriotic feeling. Render it aloud in deliberate and thoughtful style.

7. Particularly observe the judicial clearness of this example. Note the felicitous use of language.

8. Read this aloud for oratorical style. Fit the words to your lips. Engrave the passage on your mind by frequent repetition.

9. Study this passage for its profound and prophetic thought. Render it aloud in slow and dignified style.

10. Practise this for its sustained power. The words "let him" should be intensified at each repetition, and the phrase "and show me the man" brought out prominently.

11. Study this for its beauty and variety of language. Meditate upon it as a model of what a speaker should be.

12. Note the strength in the repeated phrase "I will never say." Observe the power, nobility and courage manifest throughout. The closing sentence should be read in a deeply earnest tone and at a gradually slower rate.

13. Read this for its purity and strength of style. Note the effective use of question and answer.

14. Study this passage for its common sense and exalted thought. Note how each sentence is rounded out into fulness, until it is imprest upon your memory.

EXTRACTS FOR STUDY

Specimens Of Eloquence

A Study in Climax

1. My lords, these are the securities which we have in all the constituent parts of the body of this House.

We know them, we reckon them, rest upon them, and commit safely the interests of India and of humanity into your hands. Therefore it is with confidence that, ordered by the Commons,

I impeach him in the name of all the Commons of Great Britain in Parliament assembled, whose parliamentary trust he has betrayed.

I impeach him in the name of the Commons of Great Britain, whose national character he has dishonored.

I impeach him in the name of the people of India, whose laws, rights, and liberties he has subverted, whose properties he has destroyed, whose country he has laid waste and desolate.

I impeach him in the name and by virtue of those eternal laws of justice which he has violated.

I impeach him in the name of human nature itself, which he has cruelly outraged, injured, and opprest in both sexes, in every age, rank, situation, and condition of life.—*Impeachment of Warren Hastings:* EDMUND BURKE.

Suggestions to the Public Speaker

2. I am now requiring not merely great preparation while the speaker is learning his art but after he has accomplished his education. The most splendid effort of the most mature orator will be always finer for being previously elaborated with much care. There is, no doubt, a charm in extemporaneous elocution, derived from the appearance of artless, unpremeditated effusion, called forth by the occasion, and so adapting itself to its exigencies, which

may compensate the manifold defects incident to this kind of composition: that which is inspired by the unforeseen circumstances of the moment, will be of necessity suited to those circumstances in the choice of the topics, and pitched in the tone of the execution, to the feelings upon which it is to operate. These are great virtues: it is another to avoid the besetting vice of modern oratory—the overdoing everything—the exhaustive method—which an off-hand speaker has no time to fall into, and he accordingly will take only the grand and effective view; nevertheless, in oratorical merit, such effusions must needs be very inferior; much of the pleasure they produce depends upon the hearer's surprize that in such circumstances anything can be delivered at all, rather than upon his deliberate judgment, that he has heard anything very excellent in itself. We may rest assured that the highest reaches of the art, and without any necessary sacrifice of natural effect, can only be attained by him who well considers, and maturely prepares, and oftentimes sedulously corrects and refines his oration. Such preparation is quite consistent with the introduction of passages prompted by the occasion, nor will the transition from one to the other be perceptible in the execution of the practised master.—*Inaugural Discourse:* LORD BROUGHAM.

A Study in Fervent Appeal

3. It is in vain, sir, to extenuate the matter. Gentlemen may cry, peace, peace—but there is no peace. The war is actually begun! The next gale that sweeps from the north will bring to our ears the clash of resounding arms! Our brethren are already in the field! Why stand we here idle? What is it that gentlemen wish? What would they have? Is life so dear

or peace so sweet, as to be purchased at the price of chains and slavery? Forbid it, Almighty God! I know not what course others may take, but as for me, give me liberty, or give me death!—*The War Inevitable:* PATRICK HENRY.

A Study in Dignity and Style

4. In retiring as I am about to do, forever, from the Senate, suffer me to express my heartfelt wishes that all the great and patriotic objects of the wise framers of our Constitution may be fulfilled; that the high destiny designed for it may be fully answered; and that its deliberations, now and hereafter, may eventuate in securing the prosperity of our beloved country, in maintaining its rights and honor abroad, and upholding its interests at home. I retire, I know, at a period of infinite distress and embarrassment. I wish I could take my leave of you under more favorable auspices; but without meaning at this time to say whether on any or on whom reproaches for the sad condition of the country should fall, I appeal to the Senate and to the world to bear testimony to my earnest and continued exertions to avert it, and to the truth that no blame can justly attach to me.—*Farewell Address:* HENRY CLAY.

A Study in Strength and Diction

5. For myself, I believe there is no limit fit to be assigned to it by the human mind, because I find at work everywhere, on both sides of the Atlantic, under various forms and degrees of restriction on the one hand, and under various degrees of motive and stimulus on the other, in these branches of the common race, the great principle of the freedom

of human thought, and the respectability of individual character. I find everywhere an elevation of the character of man as man, an elevation of the individual as a component part of society. I find everywhere a rebuke of the idea that the many are made for the few, or that government is anything but an agency for mankind. And I care not beneath what zone, frozen, temperate, or torrid; I care not of what complexion, white, or brown; I care not under what circumstances of climate or cultivation—if I can find a race of men on an inhabited spot of earth whose general sentiment it is, and whose general feeling it is, that government is made for man—man, as a religious, moral, and social being—and not man for government, there I know that I shall find prosperity and happiness.—*The Landing at Plymouth:* DANIEL WEBSTER.

A Study in Patriotic Feeling

6. Friends, fellow citizens, free, prosperous, happy Americans! The men who did so much to make you are no more. The men who gave nothing to pleasure in youth, nothing to repose in age, but all to that country whose beloved name filled their hearts, as it does ours, with joy, can now do no more for us; nor we for them. But their memory remains, we will cherish it; their bright example remains, we will strive to imitate it; the fruit of their wise counsels and noble acts remains, we will gratefully enjoy it.

They have gone to the companions of their cares, of their dangers, and their toils. It is well with them. The treasures of America are now in heaven. How long the list of our good, and wise, and brave, assembled there! How few remain with us! There is our Washington; and those who followed him in their country's confidence are now met together with him and all that illustrious company.—*Adams and Jefferson:* EDWARD EVERETT.

A Study in Clearness of Expression

7. I can not leave this life and character without selecting and dwelling a moment on one or two of his traits, or virtues, or felicities, a little longer. There is a collective impression made by the whole of an eminent person's life, beyond, and other than, and apart from, that which the mere general biographer would afford the means of explaining. There is an influence of a great man derived from things indescribable, almost, or incapable of enumeration, or singly insufficient to account for it, but through which his spirit transpires, and his individuality goes forth on the contemporary generation. And thus, I should say, one grand tendency of his life and character was to elevate the whole tone of the public mind. He did this, indeed, not merely by example. He did it by dealing, as he thought, truly and in manly fashion with that public mind. He evinced his love of the people not so much by honeyed phrases as by good counsels and useful service, *vera pro gratis.* He showed how he appreciated them by submitting sound arguments to their understandings, and right motives to their free will. He came before them, less with flattery than with instruction; less with a vocabulary larded with the words humanity and philanthropy, and progress and brotherhood, than with a scheme of politics, an educational, social and governmental system, which would have made them prosperous, happy and great.—*On the Death of Daniel Webster:* RUFUS CHOATE.

A Study of Oratorical Style

8. And yet this small people—so obscure and out-cast in condition—so slender in numbers and in means—so entirely unknown to the proud and great—so absolutely without name in contemporary records—whose departure from the Old World took little more than the breath of their bodies—are now illustrious beyond the lot of men; and the Mayflower is immortal beyond the Grecian Argo or the stately ship of any victorious admiral. Tho this was little foreseen in their day, it is plain now how it has come to pass. The highest greatness surviving time and storm is that which proceeds from the soul of man. Monarchs and cabinets, generals and admirals, with the pomp of courts and the circumstance of war, in the gradual lapse of time disappear from sight; but the pioneers of truth, the poor and lowly, especially those whose example elevates human nature and teaches the rights of man, so that government of the people, by the people, and for the people shall not perish from the earth, such harbingers can never be forgotten, and their renown spreads coextensive with the cause they served.—*The Qualities that Win:* CHARLES SUMNER.

A Study in Profound Thinking

9. There is something greater in the age than its greatest men; it is the appearance of a new power in the world, the appearance of the multitude of men on the stage where as yet the few have acted their parts alone. This influence is to endure to the end of time. What more of the present is to survive? Perhaps much of which we now fail to note. The glory of an age is often hidden from itself. Perhaps some word has been spoken in our day which we have not de-

signed to hear, but which is to grow clearer and louder through all ages. Perhaps some silent thinker among us is at work in his closet whose name is to fill the earth. Perhaps there sleeps in his cradle some reformer who is to move the church and the world, who is to open a new era in history, who is to fire the human soul with new hope and new daring. What else is to survive the age? That which the age has little thought of, but which is living in us all; I mean the soul, the immortal spirit. Of this all ages are the unfoldings, and it is greater than all. We must not feel, in the contemplation of the vast movements in our own and former times, as if we ourselves were nothing. I repeat it, we are greater than all. We are to survive our age, to comprehend it, and to pronounce its sentence.—*The Present Age:* W. E. CHANNING.

A Study of Sustained Power

10. Now, blue-eyed Saxon, proud of your race, go back with me to the commencement of the century, and select what statesman you please. Let him be either American or European; let him have a brain the result of six generations of culture; let him have the ripest training of university routine; let him add to it the better education of practical life; crown his temples with the silver locks of seventy years, and show me the man of Saxon lineage for whom his most sanguine admirer will wreathe a laurel, rich as embittered foes have placed on the brow of this negro,—rare military skill, profound knowledge of human nature, content to blot out all party distinctions, and trust a state to the blood of its sons,—anticipating Sir Robert Peel fifty years, and taking his station by the side of Roger Williams, before any Englishman or American had won the right;

and yet this is the record which the history of rival states makes up for this inspired black of St. Domingo.—*Toussaint L'Ouverture:* WENDELL PHILLIPS.

Study in Beauty of Language

11. He faced his audience with a tranquil mien and a beaming aspect that was never dimmed. He spoke, and in the measured cadence of his quiet voice there was intense feeling, but no declamation, no passionate appeal, no superficial and feigned emotion. It was simple colloquy—a gentleman conversing. Unconsciously and surely the ear and heart were charmed. How was it done?—Ah! how did Mozart do it, how Raffael?

The secret of the rose's sweetness, of the bird's ecstacy, of the sunset's glory—that is the secret of genius and of eloquence. What was heard, what was seen, was the form of noble manhood, the courteous and self-possest tone, the flow of modulated speech, sparkling with matchless richness of illustration, with apt allusion and happy anecdote and historic parallel, with wit and pitiless invective, with melodious pathos, with stinging satire, with crackling epigram and limpid humor, like the bright ripples that play around the sure and steady prow of the resistless ship. Like an illuminated vase of odors, he glowed with concentrated and perfumed fire. The divine energy of his conviction utterly possest him, and his

> "Pure and eloquent blood
> Spoke in his cheek, and so distinctly wrought,
> That one might almost say his body thought."

Was it Pericles swaying the Athenian multitude? Was it Apollo breathing the music of the morning from his lips?—No, no! It was an American patriot, a modern son of liberty, with a soul as firm and as true as was ever consecrated to unselfish duty, pleading with the American conscience for the chained and speechless victims of American inhumanity.—*Eulogy of Wendell Phillips:* GEORGE WILLIAM CURTIS.

A Study in Powerful Delivery

12. I thank you very cordially, both friends and opponents, if opponents you be, for the extreme kindness with which you have heard me. I have spoken, and I must speak in very strong terms of the acts done by my opponents. I will never say that they did it from passion; I will never say that they did it from a sordid love of office; I have no right to use such words; I have no right to entertain such sentiments; I repudiate and abjure them; I give them credit for patriotic motives—I give them credit for those patriotic motives which are incessantly and gratuitously denied to us. I believe we are all united in a fond attachment to the great country to which we belong; to the great empire which has committed to it a trust and function from Providence, as special and remarkable as was ever entrusted to any portion of the family of man. When I speak of that trust and that function I feel that words fail. I can not tell you what I think of the nobleness of the inheritance which has descended upon us, of the sacredness of the duty of maintaining it. I will not condescend to make it a part of controversial politics. It is a part of my being, of my flesh and blood, of my heart and soul. For those ends I have labored through my youth and manhood, and, more than that, till my hairs are gray. In that faith and practise I have lived, and

in that faith and practise I shall die.—*Midlothian Speech:* WILLIAM EWART GLADSTONE.

A Study in Purity of Style

13. Is this a reality? or is your Christianity a romance? is your profession a dream? No, I am sure that your Christianity is not a romance, and I am equally sure that your profession is not a dream. It is because I believe this that I appeal to you with confidence, and that I have hope and faith in the future. I believe that we shall see, and at no very distant time, sound economic principles spreading much more widely among the people; a sense of justice growing up in a soil which hitherto has been deemed unfruitful; and, which will be better than all—the churches of the United Kingdom—the churches of Britain awaking, as it were, from their slumbers, and girding up their loins to more glorious work, when they shall not only accept and believe in the prophecy, but labor earnestly for its fulfilment, that there shall come a time—a blessed time—a time which shall last forever—when "nation shall not lift up sword against nation, neither shall they learn war any more."—*Peace:* JOHN BRIGHT.

A Study in Common Sense and Exalted Thought

14. My countrymen, one and all, think calmly and well upon this whole subject. Nothing valuable can be lost by taking time. If there be an object to hurry any of you in hot haste to a step which you would never take deliberately, that object will be frustrated by taking time; but no good object can be frustrated by it. Such of you as are now dissatisfied still have the old Constitution unimpaired, and on the sensitive point, the laws of your own framing

under it; while the new administration will have no immediate power, if it would, to change either. If it were admitted that you who are dissatisfied hold the right side in this dispute there is still no single good reason for precipitate action. Intelligence, patriotism, Christianity, and a firm reliance on Him who has never yet forsaken this favored land are still competent to adjust in the best way all our present difficulty. In your hands, my dissatisfied fellow countrymen, and not in mine, are the momentous issues of civil war. The government will not assail you. You can have no conflict without being yourselves the aggressors. You have no oath registered in heaven to destroy the government, while I shall have the most solemn one to "preserve, protect, and defend" it.—*The First Inaugural Address:* ABRAHAM LINCOLN.

How to Speak in Public[1]

by Grenville Kleiser

The art of public speaking is so simple that it is diffi-cult. There is an erroneous impression that in order to make a successful speech a man must have unusual natural talent in addition to long and arduous study.

Consequently, many a person, when asked to make a speech, is immediately subjected to a feeling of fear or depression. Once committed to the undertaking, he spends anxious days and sleepless nights in men-tal agony, much as a criminal is said to do just prior to his execution. When at last he attempts his "maiden effort," he is almost wholly unfit for his task because of the needless waste of thought and energy expended in fear.

Elbert Hubbard once confided to me that when he made deliberate preparation for an elaborate speech,—which was seldom,—it was invariably a disappointment. To push a great speech before him for an hour or more used up most of his vitality. It was like making a speech while attempting to carry a heavy burden on the back.

1   A talk given before The Public Speaking Club of America.

How the Speaker Must Prepare Himself

There is, of course, certain preparation necessary for effective public speaking. The so-called impromptu speech is largely the product of previous knowledge and study. What the speaker has read, what he has seen, what he has heard,—in short, what he actually knows, furnishes the available material for his use.

As the public speaker gains in experience, however, he learns to put aside, at the time of speaking, all conscious thought of rules or methods. He learns through discipline how to abandon himself to the subject in hand and to give spontaneous expression to all his powers.

Primarily, then, the public speaker should have a well-stored mind. He should have mental culture in a broad way; sound judgment, a sense of proportion, mental alertness, a retentive memory, tact, and common sense,—these are vital to good speaking.

The physical requirements of the public speaker comprise good health and bodily vigor. He must have power of endurance, since there will be at times arduous demands upon him. It is worthy of note that most of the world's great orators have been men with great animal vitality.

The student of public speaking should give careful attention to his personal appearance, which includes care of the teeth. His clothes, linen, and the evidence of general care and cleanliness, will play an important part in the impression he makes upon an audience.

Elocutionary training is essential. Daily drill in deep breathing, articulation, pronunciation, voice culture, gesture, and expression, are prerequisites to polished speech. Experienced public speakers of the best type know the necessity for daily practise.

The mental training of the public speaker, so often neglected, should be regular and thorough. A reliable memory and a vivid imagination are his indispensable allies.

The moral side of the public speaker will include the development of character, sympathy, self-confidence and kindred qualities. To be a leader of other men, a speaker must have clear, settled, vigorous views upon the subject under consideration.

So much, briefly, as to the previous preparation of the speaker.

How the Speaker Must Prepare his Speech

As to the speech itself, the speaker first chooses a subject. This will depend upon the nature of the occasion and the purpose in view. He proceeds intelligently to gather material on his selected theme, supplementing the resources of his own mind with information from books, periodicals, and other sources.

The next step is to make a brief, or outline of his subject. A brief is composed of three parts, called the introduction, the discussion or statement of facts, and the conclusion. Principal ideas are placed under headings and subheadings.

The speaker next writes out his speech in full, using the brief as the basis of procedure. The discipline of writing out a speech, even tho the intention is to speak without notes, is of inestimable value. It is one of the best indications of the speaker's thoroughness and sincerity.

When the speech has at last been carefully written out, revised, and approved, should it be committed word for word to memory, or only in part, or should the speaker read from the manuscript?

The Part Memory Plays in Public Speaking

Here circumstances must govern. *The most approved method is to fix the thoughts clearly in mind, and to trust to the time of speaking for exact phraseology.* This method requires, however, that the speaker rehearse his speech over and over again, changing the form of the words frequently, so as to acquire facility in the use of language.

The great objection to memoriter speaking is that it limits and handicaps the speaker. He is like a schoolboy "saying his piece." He is in constant danger of running off the prescribed track and of having to begin again at some definite point.

The most effective speaker to-day is the one who can think clearly and promptly on his feet, and can speak from his personality rather than from his memory. Untrammelled by manuscript or effort of memory, he gives full and spontaneous expression to his powers. On the other hand, a speech from memory is like a recitation, almost inevitably stilted and artificial in character.

The Study of Words and Ideas

Those who would become highly proficient in public speaking should form the dictionary habit. It is a profitable and pleasant exercise to study lists of words and to incorporate them in one's daily conversation. Ten minutes devoted regularly every day to this study will build the vocabulary in a rapid manner.

The study of words is really a study of ideas,—since words are symbols of ideas,—and while the student is increasing his working vocabulary, in the way indicated, he is at the same time furnishing his mind with new and useful ideas.

One of the best exercises for the student of public speaking is to read aloud daily, taking care to read as he would speak. He should choose one of the standard writers, such as Stevenson, Ruskin, Newman, or Carlyle, and while reading severely criticize his delivery. Such reading should be done standing up and as if addressing an audience. This simple exercise will, in the course of a few weeks, yield the most gratifying results.

It is true that "All art must be preceded by a certain mechanical expertness," but as the highest art is to conceal art, a student must learn eventually to abandon thought of "exercises" and "rules."

Essential Qualities of the Public Speaker

The three greatest qualities in a successful public speaker are simplicity, directness, and deliberateness.

Lincoln had these qualities in preeminent degree. His speech at Gettysburg—the model short speech of all history—occupied about three minutes in delivery. Edward Everett well said afterward that he would have been content to make the same impression in three hours which Lincoln made in that many minutes.

The great public speakers in all times have been earnest and diligent students. We are familiar with the indefatigable efforts of Demosthenes, who rose from very ordinary circumstances, and goaded by the realization of great natural defects, through assiduous self-training eventually made the greatest of the world's orations, "The Speech on the Crown."

Cicero was a painstaking disciple of the speaker's art and gave himself much to the discipline of the pen. His masterly work on oratory in which he commends others to write much, remains unsurpassed to this day.

John Bright, the eminent British orator, always required time for preparation. He read every morning from the Bible, from which he drew rich material for argument and illustration. A remarkable thing about him was that he spoke seldom.

Phillips Brooks was an ideal speaker, combining simplicity and sympathy in large degree. He was a splendid type of pulpit orator produced by broad spiritual culture.

Henry Ward Beecher had unique powers as a dramatic and eloquent speaker. In his youth he hesitated in his speech, which led him to study elocution. He himself tells of how he went to the woods daily to practise vocal exercises.

He was an exponent of thorough preparation, never speaking upon a subject until he had made it his own by diligent study. Like Phillips Brooks, he was a man of large sympathy and imagination—two faculties indispensable to persuasive eloquence.

It was his oratory that first brought fame to Gladstone. He had a superb voice, and he possest that fighting force essential to a great public debater. When he quitted the House of Commons in his eighty-fifth year his powers of eloquence were practically unimpaired.

Wendell Phillips was distinguished for his personality, conversational style, and thrilling voice. He had a wonderful vocabulary, and a personal magnetism which won men instantly to him. It is said that he relied principally upon the power of truth to make his speaking eloquent. He, too, was an untiring student of the speaker's art.

As we examine the lives and records of eminent speakers of other days, we are imprest with the fact that they were sincere and earnest students of the art in which they ultimately excelled.

Learning to Think on Your Feet

One of the best exercises for learning to think and speak on the feet is to practise daily giving one minute impromptu talks upon chosen subjects. A good plan is to write subjects of a general character, on say fifty or more cards, and then to speak on each subject as it is chosen.

This simple exercise will rapidly develop facility of thought and expression and give greatly increased self-confidence.

It is a good plan to prepare more material than one intends to use—at least twice as much. It gives a comfortable feeling of security when one stands before an audience, to know that if some of the prepared matter evades his memory, he still has ample material at his ready service.

There is no more interesting and valuable study than that of speaking in public. It confers distinct advantages by way of improved health, through special exercise in deep breathing and voice culture; by way of stimulated thought and expression; and by an increase of self-confidence and personal power.

Men and women in constantly increasing numbers are realizing the importance of public speaking, and as questions multiply for debate and solution the need for this training will be still more widely appreciated, so that a practical knowledge of public speaking will in time be considered indispensable to a well-rounded education.

SPEECH FOR STUDY, WITH LESSON TALK

The Style of Theodore Roosevelt

The speeches of Mr. Roosevelt commend themselves to the student of public speaking for their fearlessness, frankness, and robustness of thought. His aim was deliberate and effective.

His style was generally exuberant, and the note of personal assertion prominent. He was direct in diction, often vehement in feeling, and one of his characteristics was a visible satisfaction when he drove home a special thought to his hearers.

It is hoped that the extract reprinted here, from Mr. Roosevelt's famous address, "The Strenuous Life," will lead the student to study the speech in its entirety. The speech will be found in "Essays and Addresses," published by The Century Company.

THE STRENUOUS LIFE[2]

By Theodore Roosevelt

In speaking to you, men of the greatest city of the West, men of the State which gave to the country Lincoln and Grant, men who preeminently and distinctly embody all that is most American in the American character, I wish to preach, not the doctrine of ignoble ease, but the doctrine of the strenuous life, the life of toil and effort, of labor and strife; to preach that highest form of success which comes, not to the man who desires mere easy peace, but to the man who does not shrink from danger, from hardship, or from bitter toil, and who out of these wins the splendid ultimate triumph.

A life of slothful ease, a life of that peace which springs merely from lack either of desire or of power to strive after great things, is as little worthy of a nation as of an individual. I ask only that what every self-respecting American demands from himself and his sons shall be demanded of the American nation as a whole. Who among you would teach the boys that ease, that peace, is to be the first consideration in their eyes—to be the ultimate goal after which they strive? You men of Chicago have made this city great, you men of Illinois have done your share, and more than your share, in making America great, because you neither preach nor practise such a doctrine. You work, yourselves, and you bring up your sons to work. If you are rich and are worth your salt you will teach your sons that tho they may have leisure, it is not to be spent in idleness; for wisely used leisure merely means that those who possess it, being free from the necessity of working for their live-

2   Extract from speech before the Hamilton Club, Chicago, April 10, 1899. From the "Strenuous Life. Essays and Addresses" by Theodore Roosevelt. The Century Co., 1900.

lihood, are all the more bound to carry on some kind of non-remunerative work in science, in letters, in art, in exploration, in historical research—work of the type we most need in this country, the successful carrying out of which reflects most honor upon the nation. We do not admire the man of timid peace. We admire the man who embodies victorious effort; the man who never wrongs his neighbor, who is prompt to help a friend, but who has those virile qualities necessary to win in the stern strife of actual life. It is hard to fail, but it is worse never to have tried to succeed. In this life we get nothing save by effort. Freedom from effort in the present merely means that there has been stored up effort in the past. A man can be freed from the necessity of work only by the fact that he or his fathers before him have worked to good purpose. If the freedom thus purchased is used aright and the man still does actual work tho of a different kind, whether as a writer or a general, whether in the field of politics or in the field of exploration and adventure, he shows he deserves his good fortune. But if he treats this period of freedom from the need of actual labor as a period, not of preparation, but of more enjoyment, he shows that he is simply a cumberer on the earth's surface, and he surely unfits himself to hold his own with his fellows if the need to do so should again arise. A mere life of ease is not in the end a very satisfactory life, and, above all, it is a life which ultimately unfits those who follow it for serious work in the world.

In the last analysis a healthy State can exist only when the men and women who make it up lead clean, vigorous, healthy lives; when the children are so trained that they shall endeavor, not to shirk difficulties, but to overcome them; not to seek ease, but to know how to wrest triumph from toil and risk. The man must be glad to do a man's work, to dare and endure and to labor; to keep himself, and to keep those dependent upon him. The woman must be the housewife, the helpmeet of the homemaker, the wise and fearless mother of many healthy children. In one of Daudet's powerful and melancholy books he speaks of "the fear of maternity, the haunting terror of the young wife of the present day." When such words can be truthfully written of a nation, that nation is rotten to the heart's core. When men fear work or fear righteous war, when women fear motherhood, they tremble on the brink of doom; and well it is that they should vanish from the earth, where they are fit subjects for the scorn of all men and women who are themselves strong and brave and high-minded.

As it is with the individual, so it is with the nation. It is a base untruth to say that happy is the nation that has no history. Thrice happy is the nation that has a glorious history. Far better it is to dare mighty things, to win glorious triumphs, even tho checkered by failure, than to take rank with those poor spirits who neither enjoy much nor suffer much, because they live in the gray twilight that knows not victory nor defeat. If in 1861 the men who loved the Union had believed that peace was the end of all things, and war and strife the worst of all things, and had acted up to their belief, we would have saved hundreds of lives, we would have saved hundreds of millions of dollars. Moreover, besides saving all the blood and treasure we then lavished, we would have prevented the heartbreak of many women, the dissolution of many homes, and we would have spared the country those months of gloom and shame when it seemed as if our armies marched only to defeat. We could have avoided all this suffering simply by shrinking from strife. And if we had thus avoided it, we would have shown that we were weaklings, and that we were unfit to stand among the great nations of the earth. Thank God for the iron in the blood of our fathers, the men who upheld the wisdom of Lincoln, and bore sword or rifle in the armies of Grant! Let us, the children of the men who proved themselves equal to the mighty days, let us the children of the men who carried the great Civil War to a triumphant conclusion, praise the God of our fathers that the ignoble counsels of peace were rejected; that the suffering and loss, the blackness of sorrow and despair were unflinchingly faced, and the years of strife endured; for in the end the slave was freed, the Union restored, and the mighty American republic placed once more as a helmeted queen among nations....

The Army and Navy are the sword and shield which this nation must carry if she is to do her duty among the nations of the earth—if she is not to stand merely as the China of the western hemisphere. Our proper conduct toward the tropic islands we have wrested from Spain is merely the form which our duty has taken at the moment. Of course, we are bound to handle the affairs of our own household well. We must see that there is civic good sense in our home administration of city, State and nation. We must strive for honesty in office, for honesty toward the creditors of the nation and of the individual, for the widest freedom of individual initiative where possible, and for the wisest control of individual initiative where it is hostile to the welfare of the many. But because we set our own household in order we are not thereby excused from playing our part in the great affairs of the world. A man's first duty is to his own home, but he is not thereby excused from doing his duty to the State; for if he fails in this second duty, it is under the penalty of ceasing to be a freeman. In the same way, while a nation's first duty is within its own borders it is not thereby absolved from facing its duties in the world as a whole; and if it refuses to do so, it merely forfeits

its right to struggle for a place among the peoples that shape the destiny of mankind.

I preach to you, then, my countrymen, that our country calls not for the life of ease, but for the life of strenuous endeavor. The twentieth century looms before us big with the fate of many nations. If we stand idly by, if we seek merely swollen, slothful ease and ignoble peace, if we shrink from the hard contests where men must win at hazard of their lives and at the risk of all they hold dear, then the bolder and stronger peoples will pass us by, and will win for themselves the domination of the world. Let us, therefore, boldly face the life of strife, resolute to do our duty well and manfully; resolute to uphold righteousness by deed and by word; resolute to be both honest and brave, to serve high ideals, yet to use practical methods. Above all, let us shrink from no strife, moral or physical, within or without the nation, provided we are certain that the strife is justified, for it is only through strife, through hard and dangerous endeavor, that we shall ultimately win the goal of true national greatness.

- **HOW TO DEVELOP SELF-CONFIDENCE IN SPEECH AND MANNER**

by Grenville Kleiser
Author of "How to Argue and Win."

In all fields of endeavor there are thousands of people who are forced to remain in the background because they lack self-confidence in speech and manner—the very fundamental of success. For just such people Grenville Kleiser has written his book "How to Develop Self-Confidence in Speech and Manner."

The work deals with methods of correction for self-consciousness, with manners as a power in the making of men, with the value of a cultivated and agreeable voice, with confidence in society and business. A series of suggestions is given for an every-day cultivation of these qualities.

> *"Embodies in a most encouraging and practical way all that is needed to make one who is naturally timid or fearful in speech and manner, self-poised, calm, dignified and confident of himself. It must be said that the method proposed is one of sober self-estimate and persistent effort along well considered lines of thought and action, designed to eradicate this uneasiness."—Times Dispatch, Richmond, Va.*

- ## HUMOROUS HITS
  ### AND HOW TO HOLD AN AUDIENCE

by Grenville Kleiser
Author of "How to Argue and Win."

This is a choice, new collection of effective recitations, sketches, stories, poems, monologues; the favorite numbers of world-famed humorists such as James Whitcomb Riley, Eugene Field, Mark Twain, Finley Peter Dunne, W. J. Lampton, Thomas Bailey Aldrich, Chas. Batell Loomis, Wallace Irwin, Richard Mansfield, Bill Nye, S. E. Kiser, Tom Masson, and others. It is the best book for home entertainment, and the most useful for teachers, orators, after-dinner speakers, and actors.

In this book, Mr. Kleiser also gives practical suggestions on how to deliver humorous or other selections so that they will make the strongest possible impression on the audience.

ELSIE JANIS, *the wonderful protean actress, says:—"I can not speak in too high praise of the opening remarks. If carefully read, will greatly assist. Have several books of choice selections, but I find some in 'Humorous Hits' never before published."*

by *Grenville Kleiser*

- *Inspiration and Ideals*
- *How to Build Mental Power*
- *How to Develop Self-Confidence in Speech and Manner*
- *How to Read and Declaim*
- *How to Speak in Public*
- *How to Develop Power and Personality in Speaking*
- *Great Speeches and How to Make Them*
- *How to Argue and Win*
- *Humorous Hits and How to Hold an Audience*
- *Complete Guide to Public Speaking*
- *Talks on Talking*
- *Fifteen Thousand Useful Phrases*
- *The World's Great Sermons*
- *Mail Course in Public Speaking*
- *Mail Course in Practical English*
- *How to Speak Without Notes*
- *Something to Say: How to Say It*

- *Successful Methods of Public Speaking*

- *Model Speeches for Practise*

- *The Training of a Public Speaker*

- *How to Sell Through Speech*

- *Impromptu Speeches: How to Make Them*

- *Word-Power: How to Develop It*

- *Christ: The Master Speaker*

- *Vital English for Speakers and Writers*

www.ingramcontent.com/pod-product-compliance
Lightning Source LLC
Chambersburg PA
CBHW021209020426
42331CB00003B/282